Sacred
Rest & Reset
RETREAT JOURNAL

Guidance & Inspiration for Your Personal Retreat

JILL PYLE & TONYA DARLINGTON

HAY HOUSE, INC.

Carlsbad, California • New York City

London • Sydney • New Delhi

Copyright © 2023 by Goddess Provisions

Published in the United States by: Hay House, Inc.: www.hayhouse.com® • *Published in Australia by:* Hay House Australia Pty. Ltd.: www.hayhouse.com.au • *Published in the United Kingdom by:* Hay House UK, Ltd.: www.hayhouse.co.uk • *Published in India by:* Hay House Publishers India: www.hayhouse.co.in

Cover design: Jay Kay at @creativewannabe_ and Bryn Starr Best

Interior design: Goddess Provisions and Bryn Starr Best

Interior illustrations: Jay Kay at @creativewannabe_

Photo of Jill Pyle: Nora Wendel
Photo of Tonya Darlington: Courtesy of Tonya Darlington

All rights reserved. No part of this book may be reproduced by any mechanical, photographic, or electronic process, or in the form of a phonographic recording; nor may it be stored in a retrieval system, transmitted, or otherwise copied for public or private use—other than for "fair use" as brief quotations embodied in articles and reviews—without prior written permission of the publisher.

The authors of this book do not dispense medical advice or prescribe the use of any technique as a form of treatment for physical, emotional, or medical problems without the advice of a physician, either directly or indirectly. The intent of the authors is only to offer information of a general nature to help you in your quest for emotional, physical, and spiritual well-being. In the event you use any of the information in this book for yourself, the authors and the publisher assume no responsibility for your actions.

Tradepaper ISBN: 978-1-4019-7438-1

10 9 8 7 6 5 4 3 2 1

1st edition, November 2023

Printed in China

This journal belongs to:

_____

If found, please contact:

_____

Retreat Details:

_____

Date:

_____

Location:

_____

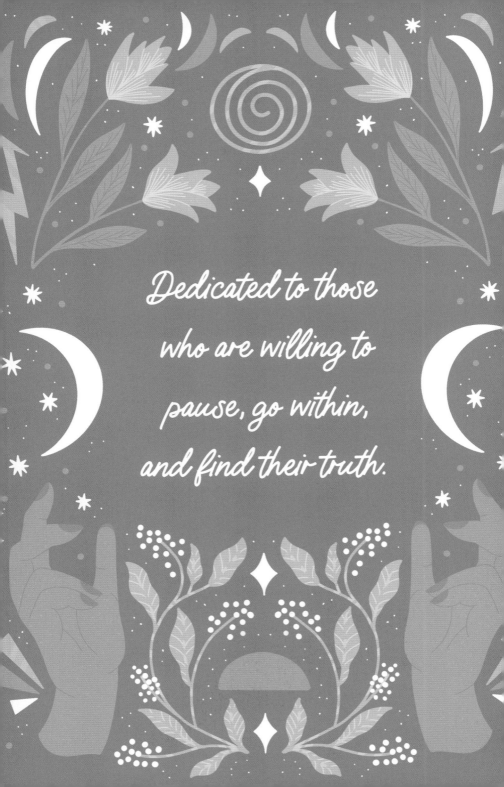

Dedicated to those
who are willing to
pause, go within,
and find their truth.

Contents

Welcome, Dear One

Going on a personal retreat can be the catalyst for life-changing transformation. Taking a few days outside of your normal schedule to go on a retreat may be the best gift you can give yourself. It doesn't require you to use up all your precious vacation days, make a huge financial commitment, travel to faraway lands, or sit with professionals. A personal retreat is a unique, intimate, and accessible option available to you right now. This planner and journal is here to be your ally in helping you create your retreat vision and offering you solace during your retreat experience.

These pages are filled with guidance and support that will inspire you to find deep, restorative rest and help you reset to discover a new sense of hope and clarity for the future. You can use it in the context of creating a space for retreat in your home or anywhere life takes you.

Your retreat can be whatever you want it to be—you're creating your reality, after all! It can be as simple as spending time unplugged from the digital world and just being you. Perhaps it's as effortless as you, nature, and a warm cup of tea. At the core, it requires making space to embrace stillness and to hear what's happening within. From this calm place, the weight you've been carrying can finally lift, which often leads to incredible moments of acceptance and inner peace.

Committing to a personal retreat experience can lead to a lot of exciting yet uncertain emotions as you plan and prepare. Breathe. Take it one moment and one page at a time.

Our Journey

First, thank you for being here and trusting us to offer guidance.

We've been close friends for nearly three decades, since growing up together in the 1990s as young women in Nova Scotia, Canada. Over the years, we have had our fair share of surprises, twists, turns, and redirections in life. Our journeys have taken us to different places on opposite sides of the planet, but our kinship has remained strong. We've always returned to doing the inner work, keeping each other accountable to our higher path, and finding joy in exchanging the aha moments and spiritual revelations that we discover during periods of rest and resets.

Rooted in love and sharing what we've learned from our often difficult growth experiences, we created this personal retreat planner and journal for you. Yes, you! We are holding the vision that you find taking a retreat to be as life-changing and transformative as we've found it. You are brave for prioritizing your rest to reset. It's within this stillness that you will undoubtedly rediscover your radiant, magnificent self.

Tonya & Jill

Where It All Began

In my early 30s, I experienced a painful and restless period of growth. For several years, I was in a deep internal struggle and exhausted from my human *doing* approach. I craved for this emotional weight I was carrying to be lifted. I knew there must be answers but didn't know where to find them. I sought answers from many professional healers, but I felt I was scratching the surface of what I needed to uncover.

My trusted Reiki Master suggested the idea of taking a personal retreat. I am forever grateful for their gentle encouragement to spend a couple of quiet days to rest and reset. I didn't know what a personal retreat was, so I searched online. Not finding helpful results, I had to take a leap of faith and "wing it"!

My personal retreat experience began with me, nature, and a warm cup of tea. Sitting outside a charming cabin in the woods, I took a moment of silence followed by my first deep breath in a long time. I was totally "unplugged" from the day-to-day hustle and was a human *being*! Finally, at peace in the stillness, I was feeling into my body, mind, and spirit. I filled the pages of a blank journal with thoughts that were coming up from within.

It was an incredibly life-changing and transformative experience. With no plan, I spent a weekend alone meditating, hiking, practicing yoga in the nude, making and eating delicious food, soaking in the sun on a hammock, and feeling all my feelings! I did nothing and everything all at once. It was glorious! The weight I'd been carrying lifted in the still and safe space I had created.

I came out of that experience rested, reset, and with a renewed sense of hope and clarity for the future. Through that humbling personal retreat experience, I created the foundation of what you're holding in your hands today. It is my intention that this planner and journal provides the guidance I wish I'd had when taking my first personal retreat.

From my hands, head, and heart to yours,

Tonya

PS: A special thanks to Jill and Hay House for their support in bringing this next-level incarnation of this planner and journal to life. I'm humbled to see my passion project reach its full potential and serve others.

Just Breathe

How to Rest & Reset

Planning a Personal Retreat

First and foremost, going on a retreat requires you to break the cycle of your typical daily patterns and spend time alone in a space where you can experience your thoughts and feelings in a safe and welcoming environment.

With the guidance in this planner, you can easily spend anywhere from one day to a week journaling with the inner-reflection prompts. The more time you can give yourself to reflect at a comfortable pace, the better. It would be ideal to take at least a weekend to rest and reset with a focus on your body, mind, and spirit.

Your retreat could take place at a mountain cabin, lake house, or hotel room. It could also be in your home with the proper preparation to ensure the space is a safe and welcoming environment.

This planner and journal will encourage you to reflect on your retreat vision and intention to help you determine the best personal retreat environment for your needs.

The Benefits

The magic that unfolds when you rest and reset:

- No or minimal distractions
- Refresh your nervous system
- Enjoy quiet space
- Eat and drink what you love
- Discover the power of uninterrupted *you* time
- Empower yourself to be alone, which can be a new experience for many
- Gain incredible benefits for which your body, mind, and spirit will thank you

Personal retreat experiences differ from organized retreats in that you can:

- Set your budget
- Determine your dates and location
- Decide your duration
- Create your environment
- Manage your energy
- Respect your boundaries
- Choose your activities
- Plan your agenda (or set no agenda)
- Hold yourself accountable

Common Questions About Going on a Retreat

Am I doing it right?

As long as you feel safe, there is no "wrong way" to carry out your retreat. You set your intention for your retreat and decide what to focus on or manifest. If you stick to the boundaries you've set for yourself, then you can be confident that your retreat is the best for you based on your available resources.

As an occasional retreat check-in, you can ask yourself, "At this moment, am I just being?" If the answer is yes, then carry on. If the answer is no, revisit the boundaries you set for yourself (see page 17) and readjust. Simple as that.

What will I do on my retreat?

The answer is simple: You do "nothing," yet everything will begin happening for you. Don't overthink it. The idea is to be. Clarity will unfold before you in the stillness.

What if I've never been on a retreat?

You don't have to do it all, accomplish it all, discover it all, or resolve it all. You may not have many big revelations, but even a small insight of self-awareness can have a lasting impact.

What is important is to be clear with your intentions and to commit to the boundaries you have set. Let the rest unfold naturally!

Retreating Responsibly

This *Sacred Rest & Reset Retreat Journal* has been shared with you because we wholeheartedly believe it can support your inner guidance in a beautiful and positive way. The planner section considers your safety and deeply encourages you to share your personal retreat plan with a trusted friend. It is important to understand yourself and intuitively know if this is an experience where you will feel physically and psychologically safe. Please respect your own boundaries and limits. Trust your instincts and know that pausing or ending your retreat at any time is always an available option. Ultimately your personal retreat experience is your responsibility. Please practice good decision-making to ensure your own safety and well-being.

PLANNER

Before Your Retreat

Planning Your Retreat

Timing: A week or more before your retreat, take a couple of hours to reflect and complete the planning pages in this section. This is the time to consider the different elements of your upcoming retreat. Reflect on what type of space you need to surround yourself with so you can fully embrace the experience and minimize distractions. Preparing for a smooth experience will support your nervous system when the retreat begins so you can relax and go deep.

To prepare, you can review and complete the following sections:

- Visualization
- Activity Inspiration
- Setting Your Boundaries
- Sharing with a Trusted Friend
- Retreat Preparation Checklist
- Retreat Details

Visualization

Your retreat will be a unique journey customized by you for you. Before diving into planning, take a moment to go within to visualize what you want your experience to be like and to clarify how you would like to feel on your retreat. Once you have a general sense of this, you can better plan your experience.

Guided Visualization

Get cozy by sitting or lying down in a quiet place where you feel comfortable. This could be in the bathtub, on your bed, in a favorite chair, outside beneath the trees, or near water. Take a few long, deep breaths and set a five-minute timer. Close your eyes and visualize walking through the front door of your personal retreat and pay attention to what it feels like to be in this space. Consider the following questions within your visualization, and jot down notes after you feel complete.

Where were you?

_____

_____

What time of year was it (spring, summer, fall, winter)?

_____

What was the weather like?

_____

_____

What did the space look like?

_____

_____

How did you feel in your body?

_____

_____

What activities were you enjoying?

_____

_____

What food and drink were you nourishing yourself with?

_____

_____

What were you wearing?

_____

_____

What were you reflecting on?

_____

_____

What were you appreciating?

_____

_____

How many days did you enjoy this experience, and why is this the perfect timing for you?

_____

One word to describe your visualization:

_____

Activity Inspiration

The main focus of a personal retreat experience is simply to just *be*. That said, you may want to plan some activities, as listed in this section, that will start to spark your inspiration.

Allow your intuition to guide you to the activities that will be the most beneficial and illuminating for you. After each activity, take time to journal and capture any insights.

ART

Tap into your inner creatrix by getting artsy. Consider drawing, painting, or doodling to express your creativity. You can use nature as your canvas and collect leaves, stack rocks, or draw in the earth with a stick. Take a look at your environment and tap into your inner resourcefulness!

BODY SCAN

While sitting, standing, or lying down, visualize checking in mentally to every inch of your internal and external body, starting from your toes and working your way up your body. Pay attention to what you are feeling within. Take time to be with each part of your body, each organ. Focus on releasing and relaxing any tension. Be sure to breathe deeply and go slowly. You may be surprised to learn what messages your body has in store for you!

FOREST BATHING

Go for a walk to explore the natural environment. If you've been to the surrounding area before, try to explore it in a new way and with fresh eyes. Remove your shoes and feel the ground beneath you. Soak up all the positive energy you can from the nature surrounding you. Connect to your senses. What do you see, hear, feel, taste, and smell? How does it feel to connect to all your senses and the Earth?

MEDITATION

Sit or lay down in a quiet spot and begin to observe your breath. Breathe in for 5 seconds and out for 10 seconds to slow down your nervous system and mental chatter. When you notice a thought, put it in a balloon and imagine it floating away. The idea is to just be and observe what thoughts arise without judging, labeling or attaching to them in any way.

MOVE YOUR BODY

What does your body need right now? To dance? To exercise? To jump? To stretch? In comfortable clothing (or in the nude!), take a moment to close your eyes and feel into your body. Start with small, subtle movements and then intuitively move your body in a way that feels nourishing.

PLAY

If you enjoy games, then this activity is for you. Ideally, find a way to play that doesn't involve your phone or computer. You may need to be a bit creative but see what you can come up with. This could be kicking a ball around the yard, throwing a ball at a target, or playing a round of solitaire with a physical card deck. Take some time to just play a little in your life.

PLEASURE

Take a moment to reflect on what a pleasurable experience truly is for you. Is it a long, hot bath? Reading a book? Napping in a hammock? Playing an instrument? A foot massage? Perhaps it is something more sensual and intimate. Whatever it is, take time to prioritize a pleasurable experience.

POETRY

Connect to your inner poet. Put pen to paper and see what arises. Poetry has no rules, and it can be therapeutic to write down thoughts, observations, or confessions in a way that is not restricted to the formalities of sentence structures. You could try writing to someone or yourself, writing about what you observe around you, or digging deep into your subconscious to see what unfolds.

REST

This journal is called *Sacred Rest & Reset* so absolutely please prioritize your rest! Take a cozy afternoon nap or lie down near a window (better yet get outside) to feel the warmth of the sun on your skin. Rest is always available to you and we highly encourage lots of it as you enjoy your personal retreat.

SEND LOVE

Is there someone in your life who could use extra love, support, and positive affirmation? Take a moment to hold space for them, sending an abundance of loving energy by visualizing your hearts connected with a golden cord of light. Alternatively or in addition, you can write them a letter. Depending on the situation, you can give them the letter or burn it to release the energy into the ether.

STARGAZING

There is nothing more humbling than looking into that deep midnight sky and watching the stars, moon, and planets. Allow yourself to gaze into the abyss and to feel into what comes up for you.

VOICE

Our voice is a power center for healing on all levels. Try speaking or singing your thoughts out loud. You could make up a song or dig deep into your gut and release intuitive tones and sounds from within. Don't worry about making beautiful or complex sounds or songs; you can keep it as simple as you like. One excellent option is to chant and vibrate with the sound of "om."

Setting Your Boundaries

Committing to a personal retreat experience requires you to consider setting boundaries with yourself and others to ensure you have the most meaningful experience possible. Consider what boundaries you may want to set for yourself and what you need to communicate to others. For example, you may choose not to use your phone or to follow a special meal plan.

Indicate below the boundaries that you are setting for your personal retreat experience.

☐ Alcohol-free

☐ Audio-free

☐ Caffeine-free

☐ Clocks/time tracking-free

☐ Communications-free

☐ Dairy-free

☐ Device-free

☐ Drug-free

☐ Internet-free

☐ Meat-free

☐ Reading-free

☐ Sugar-free

☐ Television-free

☐ Other: _____

☐ Other: _____

☐ Other: _____

☐ Other: _____

Reflect on and note actions and/or communications needed to set and hold these boundaries with yourself and others.

_____

_____

_____

_____

_____

_____

Sharing with a Trusted Friend

It's so important for you to feel supported and safe. Please consider sharing your retreat plans with a trusted friend, loved one, or family member. If you desire, they could take on the role of your accountability partner and support you after your retreat in realizing your actionable insights, too.

MY TRUSTED FRIEND IS:

This is a person you'll ask to encourage you with love and support prior to your retreat and help hold you accountable in following through with your actionable insights after your retreat.

Share the following with your trusted friend, along with any other important details you want them to know:

- ☐ Retreat dates
- ☐ Retreat location and host contact information, if applicable
- ☐ When they can expect to hear from you next
- ☐ How to reach you, if needed
- ☐ Any other important details

Retreat Preparation Checklist

List any other to-dos you feel you need to complete so that you can be in the present moment during your retreat and capture your packing list below:

- [ ] _____
- [ ] _____
- [ ] _____
- [ ] _____
- [ ] _____
- [ ] _____
- [ ] _____
- [ ] _____
- [ ] _____
- [ ] _____
- [ ] _____
- [ ] _____
- [ ] _____
- [ ] _____
- [ ] _____
- [ ] _____
- [ ] _____
- [ ] _____
- [ ] _____

Retreat Details

RETREAT NAME:

For example, Tonya's Silent Retreat

_____

RETREAT TYPE:

For example, self-guided personal retreat, self-guided couples/group retreat, organized retreat

_____

DATES:

_____

LOCATION/ACCOMMODATION:

_____

TRANSPORTATION/TRAVEL PLAN:

_____

DATES OFF WORK:

_____

CHILDCARE AND/OR PET CARE PLAN:

_____

TRUSTED FRIEND/ACCOUNTABILITY PARTNER:

_____

The most important

work we can do is

the work we do

on ourselves.

OPENING CEREMONY

Stepping into Your Retreat

Welcome to Your Retreat

Timing: The first few hours of your retreat.

After you arrive at your destination, it is essential to ease into your retreat, as it can take a bit of time to transition from the environment you are leaving and fully arrive within your retreat space. Even if you haven't changed physical locations and are doing a home retreat, an energetic shift will take place. Take a moment to breathe and complete the opening activities suggested in the following sections.

In the retreat opening pages, you will find:

- Opening Check-In
- Opening Ritual
- Opening Ritual Reflections
- Opening Love Letter
- One-Word Opener

Opening Check-In

Once you arrive at your retreat destination, or you have officially started your retreat if you're staying at home, go through the following checklist to make sure you have a safe space and have established the boundaries of your retreat.

Within the first day of your retreat, confirm you have:

- ☐ Communicated personal retreat experience plans and boundaries with friends/family

- ☐ Turned off your phone (and made sure it is charged)

- ☐ Turned off or removed clocks in the space (if you want to go into a liminal, timeless space and have no set schedule)

- ☐ Removed distractions in the space

- ☐ Explored the space to know where everything is

- ☐ Provided what's needed in terms of water and nourishment

- ☐ Unpacked and settled into the space

- ☐ Made your flashlight and emergency contact list easily accessible, if applicable

- ☐ Figured out where the fire extinguisher and first aid kit are, if applicable

- ☐ Arranged the space as needed

- ☐ Removed any clutter

- ☐ Changed into cozy clothes

- ☐ Given yourself a loving hug

- ☐ Taken a long, deep breath

Opening Ritual

Open your retreat with an intuitively selected ritual connecting you to the space, yourself, and your intention. Some potential ritual elements include:

CLEARING THE ENERGY

Burn incense or resins with cleansing herbs to clear the energy.

GROUNDING YOURSELF

Take some time outside, ground your energy, and put your bare feet on the earth.

CREATING AN ALTAR

Lay out sacred items, crystals, or personal objects that have a significant meaning to you.

SAYING AN AFFIRMATION

Speak out loud in the space, proclaiming this as your sanctuary for your retreat and what you intend to experience within this container.

SCANNING YOUR BODY

Feel your entire body from head to toe and where energy is flowing or stagnant.

BREATHING DEEPLY

Take three or more full, nourishing breaths.

MEDITATING

Sit in stillness and notice what comes up for you.

WALKING IN NATURE

In silence, walk and observe all the magnificent plants and creatures around you.

FREESTYLE

What feels like the perfect way for you to land in the retreat space and open the transformation portal?

Opening Ritual Reflections

Spend a moment feeling into your mind, spirit, and body—or your head, heart, and hands. Notice what thoughts and emotions are surfacing in each area.

Head: What thoughts are running through your mind right now? Any fears, excitements, or questions to note?

_____

_____

_____

_____

_____

Heart: How are you feeling inside? What emotions are just below the surface waiting to come up?

_____

_____

_____

_____

_____

Hands: What, if anything, do you feel needs "doing"? How does this make you feel?

_____

_____

_____

_____

_____

Opening Love Letter

Write a love letter to welcome yourself into the sacred container of your retreat experience.

Dear _____,

_____

_____

_____

_____

_____

_____

_____

_____

_____

_____

_____

_____

_____

_____

_____

_____

_____

_____

_____

_____

_____

_____

_____

_____

_____

_____

Love, _____

One-Word Opener

One word to describe how you are feeling right now:

_____

To understand yourself
is to know yourself,
is to accept yourself,
is to love yourself.

SETTING
YOUR
INTENTIONS
Beginning Your Retreat

The Power of Intention

Timing: Once you are settled and relaxed in your retreat space, take time to set intentions. This is the opportune time to get clear about the vision for your retreat and set yourself up for success.

This section is designed to help you explore your retreat objectives and set goals.

In the following pages, you will find:

- Your "Why"
- Exploring Your "Why"
- Holding Your Vision
- Defining How You Want to Feel
- Reflecting on Your Hopes and Dreams
- Creating Your Intention Statement
- Letting Go of Expectations
- Surrendering to the Unknown
- Creating Positive Affirmations
- Reviewing Your Retreat Plan

Your "Why"

From the following list, check those reasons that resonate with you as your "why" for planning this retreat:

- ☐ Crave relaxation and restoration
- ☐ Ache for the calmness of no to-do list
- ☐ Seek clarity and understanding of my path
- ☐ Dream of having dedicated space for "me time"
- ☐ Need stillness to explore life's big questions
- ☐ Require room to focus on specific projects or decisions
- ☐ Desire to explore the power of mindfulness and meditation
- ☐ Want time to focus on self-acceptance, self-love, and inner peace
- ☐ Yearn to know who I am at my core
- ☐ Dare to explore the adventure of disconnecting from my day-to-day hustle to rest and reset
- ☐ Other: _____

  _____
- ☐ Other: _____

  _____
- ☐ Other: _____

  _____
- ☐ Other: _____

  _____
- ☐ Other: _____

Exploring Your "Why"

How did you get to this place in your personal and emotional journey? How do you think having time to explore these feelings will benefit your life?

_____

_____

_____

_____

_____

_____

_____

_____

_____

_____

_____

_____

_____

_____

_____

_____

_____

_____

_____

Holding Your Vision

In short, how would you describe your vision for the retreat? How do you want to feel? What is your ideal setting?

Note: You can reference the "Guided Visualization" section (see page 12) about visualizing yourself on the retreat.

_____

_____

_____

_____

In what areas of your life do you want to gain clarity?

_____

_____

_____

_____

Why is this retreat important to you?

_____

_____

_____

_____

How will you know if your retreat was a "success"? How will you feel or what will happen to affirm this for you?

_____

_____

_____

Defining How You Want to Feel

The energy of being on a retreat can create space to safely feel:

- Connected and intuitive
- Awakened and alive
- Relaxed and restored
- Grateful and happy
- Accepted and understood
- Appreciated and respected
- Focused and motivated
- Peaceful and content
- Creative and unique
- Courageous and empowered
- Trusting and honest
- Grounded and whole
- Loved and enlightened

How do you want to feel during your retreat?

_____

_____

_____

_____

_____

_____

_____

_____

Reflecting on Your Hopes and Dreams

Review your vision and freewrite to reflect about your hopes, dreams, and intention for your retreat.

_____

_____

_____

_____

_____

_____

_____

_____

_____

_____

_____

_____

_____

_____

_____

_____

_____

_____

_____

_____

_____

_____

_____

✧ Creating Your Intention Statement ·

Having an intention statement gives you a key phrase or word that's easy to remember. It's something you can come back to throughout your retreat experience to keep yourself on track and remind you of why you set out on this journey.

MY INTENTION FOR THIS RETREAT IS:

Example: To rest; To get a fresh perspective;
To get clear about what's working for me and what's not

_____

_____

_____

_____

MY MANTRA:

Example: I am relaxing, I am figuring out
what's important to me, I am nourishing my spirit

_____

_____

_____

_____

MY KEYWORD(S):

Example: relax, peace, connection

_____

_____

_____

Letting Go of Expectations

It is important to note that even with thoughtful planning, anything can happen. This is where we encourage you to fully accept the experience for what it is and trust your retreat will unfold in a way that will be for your greatest and highest good, even if you forgot your toothbrush or the room you booked doesn't look like the photos. We encourage you to do your best not to create rigid expectations for your retreat but to embrace the mystery in your unfolding experience with openness, love, and curiosity.

What are some expectations you may be holding on to that would be helpful for you to let go?

_____

_____

_____

_____

_____

_____

_____

_____

_____

_____

_____

_____

_____

_____

Surrendering to the Unknown

At some point during your retreat, you may feel yourself brushing up against the edges of your comfort. Allow space for your fears, resistance, and uncertainties to arise and be witnessed. This simple act can allow you to see where your discomforts and fears are rooted. Give yourself the space to reflect on whether or not your fears are rational or serving you. Having the space to witness and contemplate them can help to shift your perspective and change unconscious beliefs that have been limiting you.

What fears, doubts, uncertainties, or worries do you have going into this retreat?

_____

_____

_____

_____

Where do these feelings come from?

_____

_____

_____

_____

Are you ready to release these feelings? What is your approach to letting go of these feelings?

_____

_____

_____

_____

Creating Positive Affirmations

Take a few minutes to meditate and channel some positive messages with the assistance of your guides and higher self. Try to refine your inspiration and feelings into a short statement that will be easy to repeat to yourself. You can write down some positive affirmations below that will be easy for you to reference throughout your retreat. For example, *"I'm brave/healing/always guided."*

Reviewing Your Retreat Plan

MY "WHY"

I'm taking a retreat because:

_____

_____

My desired outcome is:

_____

_____

SACRED SPACE

My retreat space allows me to feel:

_____

_____

ACTIVITIES

I am looking forward to spending time:

_____

_____

REFLECTION

It is my hope that I will also take time to reflect on:

_____

_____

POSITIVE AFFIRMATION

A mantra I can repeat to myself to keep on track:

_____

_____

JOURNAL
PROMPTS

*Guidance & Inspiration
for Your Personal Retreat*

Internal Deep Dive

Timing: Take a minimum of a weekend and up to a week for your personal retreat experience.

The following pages contain activities and journal prompts to help guide you. As you go through the pages, rest in knowing this is gentle guidance meant to support you in discovering your true inner feelings. Feel free to intuitively navigate the activities and journal prompts. Don't put any pressure on yourself to complete everything. Allow your spirit to gravitate toward what feels most relevant and impactful for your healing and growth.

In this section you will find the following prompts:

- Sacred Self-Care Wheel
- Sacred Self-Care Wheel Reflections
- Manifesting Your Future Self
- Reflecting On Your Life
- Closing the Gap
- Gratitude List
- Life Needs More . . .
- Inner Feelings
- Feeling Your Feelings
- Living Your Best Life
- Personal Values

- Happy Places
- No-Regrets Moments
- Proudest Moments
- Courageous Moments
- Self-Love
- Big Dreams
- Letting Go
- Relationship to Pleasure
- Life's Joys
- In Stillness
- Playtime
- Free-Flow Reflections

Sacred Self-Care Wheel

It's time to get real, raw, and radically honest about your life, starting with the state of your self-care practice. Self-care is one of the key pillars of your wellness and quality of life. Understanding where you are with your self-care practice can illuminate the best steps to take that will shift your life and put you on your highest path.

Self-care spans a wide range of activities, and the sacred self-care wheel is a visual representation of your current self-care practice. The following are the 11 key areas of this wheel that you can evaluate to get a holistic sense of where you're doing great and where you'd benefit from focusing more energy.

1. **Relaxation:** Bath, facial, self-massage, watching a movie, reading, walking, doing things that relax you

2. **Reflection Time:** Journaling, gratitude practice, goal setting, spending intentional time alone, organizing your thoughts, figuring out how you really feel

3. **Meditation:** Silent meditation, sound bathing, grounding work, movement meditations

4. **Nourishment:** Eating healthy food, drinking water, prioritizing your health

5. **Sleep:** Resting, napping, dreaming, creating a nest, preparing for sleep, sleeping

6. **Connect with Nature:** Being outside, connecting with plants and animals, swimming in rivers or the ocean, mapping the moon cycle

7. **Physical Wellness:** Doing yoga, exercising, keeping your body healthy, seeing a doctor or naturopath, taking helpful supplements or medicines

8. **Creative Expression:** Adorning your body, painting, writing, using your hands, singing, dancing, making music

9. **Connection with Friends, Family, and Community:** Spending quality time together, keeping in touch, sending them love, feeling unconditional love, volunteering

10. **Romantic Relationships and Pleasure:** Enjoying romantic love, having sex, self-pleasuring, doing yoni crystal work, feeling a connection to your womb space

11. **Connection to Spirit:** Listening to your intuition, manifesting, calling in your guides, conducting rituals, performing moon ceremonies, energy work, reading tarot cards, making crystal grids

Putting pen to paper and using a wheel to evaluate the different aspects of your life is a powerful way to visualize how you're doing in each area of your life.

To get started, review each of the 11 spheres of self-care and rate yourself on how well you feel you're doing in each. Rate yourself a 10 in areas where you feel fully balanced and dedicated to the sphere of self-care practice and a 1 where you don't spend any time or energy. Be gentle with yourself and be honest.

Once you rate each sphere, you can color that area on the next page. You'll unveil a clear visual representation of the state of your self-care practice. Ideally, you'd want all sections of your wheel to be colored in equally and at a high level, so like a typical wheel it would roll smoothly. If it's filled in at different levels, some high and some low, your wheel wouldn't be very functional. This would also represent imbalance in your life. When even one area of your self-care practice is ignored or lacking, it can make for a bumpy ride.

On the next page you will find an example of a completed Self-Care Wheel by a person who is still coming into balance with creating a holistic self-care routine:

Sample Sacred Self-Care Wheel

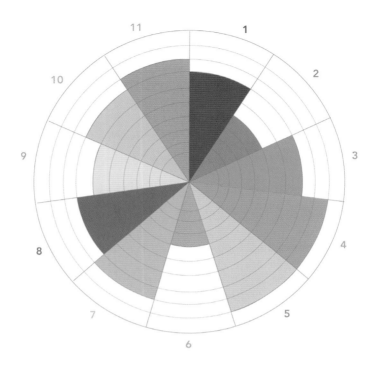

1. Relaxation — 7

2. Reflection Time — 5

3. Meditation — 7

4. Nourishment — 9

5. Sleep — 9

6. Connection with Nature — 4

7. Physical Wellness — 8

8. Creative Expression — 7

9. Connection with Friends, Family and Community — 6

10. Romantic Relationships and Pleasure — 7

11. Connection to Spirit — 8

Your Sacred Self-Care Wheel

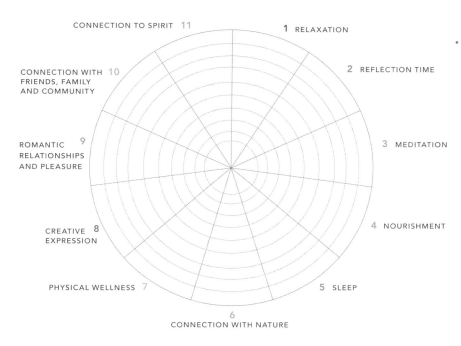

Out of 10, I rate my self-care practice in each of these categories as:

1. Relaxation — ☐
2. Reflection Time — ☐
3. Meditation — ☐
4. Nourishment — ☐
5. Sleep — ☐
6. Connection with Nature — ☐
7. Physical Wellness — ☐
8. Creative Expression — ☐
9. Connection with Friends, Family and Community — ☐
10. Romantic Relationships and Pleasure — ☐
11. Connection to Spirit — ☐

Sacred Self-Care Wheel Reflections

Which areas of self-care do you excel at?

_____

_____

_____

_____

Which areas of self-care do you want to focus on more?

_____

_____

_____

_____

_____

_____

What obstacles, real or imagined, are holding you back?

_____

_____

_____

_____

_____

_____

_____

_____

_____

Manifesting Your Future Self.

Go wild and write out the future as if it were the present: What would it look like if you were taking fantastic care of yourself, as if you've rated yourself eight or higher in every area of the self-care wheel? What would life be like if you had a holistic self-care practice? How would you feel? What could you do if you were energized, radiant, and expanded in your capacity for love?

Reflecting On Your Life

Ask yourself, "Where am I now?" and consider where you are at this current stage in life. To help you take inventory, respond to the following questions:

How would you describe your mood, and how does it fluctuate?

_____

_____

_____

_____

What thoughts and beliefs keep coming up in your head?

_____

_____

_____

_____

Have you had any major life changes recently?

_____

_____

_____

_____

Is anything currently causing you to feel stressed?

_____

_____

_____

_____

What new topics, people, or places have you found yourself becoming curious about?

_____

_____

_____

_____

What new hobbies and activities have been piquing your interest?

_____

_____

_____

_____

Have there been any consistent patterns with your dreams and/or sleep?

_____

_____

_____

_____

What aspirations have been coming up in relation to your career?

_____

_____

_____

What themes have been coming up with your physical health?

_____

_____

_____

Closing the Gap

You've reflected on where you want to be and where you are now. What "gaps" can you see, and what do you intuitively think are the next steps you need to take to start manifesting your dream life?

_____

_____

_____

_____

_____

_____

_____

_____

_____

_____

_____

_____

_____

_____

_____

_____

_____

_____

_____

_____

Being aware
of your thoughts and
feelings is powerful, but
even more powerful is how
you choose to act with
that awareness.

Gratitude List

From large to small, what are you most thankful for?

- _____
- _____
- _____
- _____
- _____
- _____
- _____
- _____
- _____

What does this gratitude list help you to realize?

_____
_____
_____
_____
_____
_____
_____
_____
_____
_____
_____
_____
_____

Life Needs More...

What are you ready to manifest?

* _____
* _____
* _____
* _____
* _____
* _____
* _____
* _____
* _____

What is your next major step to start cultivating these desires?

_____
_____
_____
_____
_____
_____
_____
_____
_____
_____
_____
_____
_____

Inner Feelings

Take a deep breath. Put one hand on your belly and one hand on your heart. Allow your belly to fully relax as you take several deep inhales and exhales. Once you're feeling relaxed, take some time to feel what sensations are arising within your body. Sit with your thoughts and listen to what is coming up for you. Tune in with yourself on a soul level to gather insight into what you're experiencing in the core of your being. Take a few minutes to write down key points about what you discover in each section below:

BODY

- _____
- _____
- _____
- _____
- _____

MIND

- _____
- _____
- _____
- _____
- _____

SPIRIT

- _____
- _____
- _____
- _____
- _____

Feeling Your Feelings

How easy or difficult is it for you to feel yourself on the level of your body, mind, and spirit? Is it possible for you to feel yourself on all levels, or are some areas more elusive? What do you think you need to do (or not do) in order to obtain even more clarity into your feelings?

Living Your Best Life

What are you doing in the morning, afternoon, and evening when you're living your best life? Describe your best life in below.

My ideal morning:

_____

_____

_____

_____

My ideal afternoon:

_____

_____

_____

My ideal evening:

_____

_____

_____

_____

My ideal weekend:

_____

_____

_____

My ideal vacation:

_____

_____

_____

_____

My ideal friend network:

_____

_____

_____

_____

My ideal income/career situation:

_____

_____

_____

_____

My ideal romantic partnership:

_____

_____

_____

_____

What practical steps can you take that are within your power to start creating your best life?

_____

_____

_____

_____

Personal Values

List the values that are most important to you in life:

- _____
- _____
- _____
- _____
- _____
- _____
- _____
- _____

What do you feel your values say about the kind of being you are?

_____
_____
_____
_____
_____
_____
_____
_____
_____
_____
_____
_____
_____
_____
_____

Happy Places

Where do you spend time that makes you feel comfortable, supported, and joyful?

- _____
- _____
- _____
- _____
- _____
- _____
- _____
- _____

How can you spend more time in or create places that make you feel uplifted and truly at home?

_____
_____
_____
_____
_____
_____
_____
_____
_____
_____
_____
_____

No-Regrets Moments

In which areas of your life have you recently made hard decisions or taken risks that led you to a positive outcome?

- _____
- _____
- _____
- _____
- _____
- _____
- _____
- _____

What helped you feel brave or confident during these pivotal decisions? Or if they were scary, how did you know you were making the right choice for you?

_____
_____
_____
_____
_____
_____
_____
_____
_____
_____
_____
_____
_____

Proudest Moments

When can you recall feeling truly proud of your accomplishments?

- _____
- _____
- _____
- _____
- _____
- _____
- _____
- _____

In moments when you have felt most proud of yourself, were you able to sustain that pride regardless of whether others validated your efforts?

_____
_____
_____
_____
_____
_____
_____
_____
_____
_____
_____
_____

Courageous Moments

When and where has your inner warrior shown up to support you in making brave choices?

- _____
- _____
- _____
- _____
- _____
- _____
- _____
- _____

Do you consider yourself a brave person? What, if anything, stands in the way of you feeling totally courageous in choosing your heart's desires?

_____
_____
_____
_____
_____
_____
_____
_____
_____
_____
_____
_____

Self-Love

You are amazing! This is the moment to gush about yourself with pure love. What are some things you love about yourself? Don't hold back—this is a full permission slip to love on yourself!

- _____
- _____
- _____
- _____
- _____
- _____
- _____

Do any beliefs or patterns stand in the way of totally loving and accepting yourself?

_____

_____

_____

_____

_____

_____

_____

_____

_____

_____

_____

_____

Big Dreams

Claim your destiny! What do you want to accomplish in this life?

- _____
- _____
- _____
- _____
- _____
- _____
- _____
- _____

What do you feel is your true purpose in this life?

_____
_____
_____
_____
_____
_____
_____
_____
_____
_____
_____
_____
_____

Hint: It's usually a unique combination of all things you're most passionate about and drawn to.

Letting Go

What are you ready to let go of?

- _____
- _____
- _____
- _____
- _____
- _____
- _____
- _____

How will your life shift if you let go of these things?

_____
_____
_____
_____
_____
_____
_____
_____
_____
_____
_____
_____
_____
_____

Relationship to Pleasure

You are so worthy of experiencing pleasure! How would you describe your relationship to sensual and sexual pleasure?

_____

_____

_____

_____

_____

_____

What feels like the next best step you can take to cultivate more pleasure in your life?

_____

_____

_____

_____

_____

What emotional or thought patterns do you notice that may be standing in your way of embracing more pleasure?

_____

_____

_____

_____

Life's Joys

What, who, or where brings you joy?

- _____
- _____
- _____
- _____
- _____
- _____
- _____
- _____

What steps could you take to cultivate more joy on a daily basis?

_____
_____
_____
_____
_____
_____
_____
_____
_____
_____
_____
_____
_____

In Stillness

What thoughts, stories, or feelings come up for you when you pause in stillness?

_____

_____

_____

_____

_____

_____

_____

_____

_____

_____

What is your comfort level with stillness? What in your life has led to these feelings of either comfort or discomfort?

_____

_____

_____

_____

_____

_____

_____

_____

_____

Playtime

When and where do you find yourself able to embrace your playful side?

- _____
- _____
- _____
- _____
- _____
- _____
- _____
- _____

Does playing feel like a good use of your time? Why or why not?

_____
_____
_____
_____
_____
_____
_____
_____
_____
_____
_____
_____
_____
_____

Free-Flow Reflections

This is your space to write whatever thoughts, ideas, questions, or feelings come up for you. Let go of all structure and any perfectionist tendencies. Just allow yourself to write what emerges without judgment.

*What appears
to be the end
is often simply
the beginning.*

CLOSING
CEREMONY
Stepping Out of Your Retreat

Completing Your Retreat.

Timing: The last hours of your retreat.

Take a moment to honor your experience and gather the gold as you create a sweet closing ceremony for yourself.

In the following pages, you will find:

- Revisit Your Intention Statement°
- Start, Stop, Stick
- Learned, Loved, Let Go
- Unanswered Questions
- Closing Ritual
- Closing Reflections
- Closing Love Letter
- Checkout Checklist
- One-Word Closer

Revisit Your Intention Statement

What was your intention for this retreat, summarized in a word or sentence (see page 37)?

_____

_____

_____

Do you feel you manifested your intention? Why or why not?

_____

_____

_____

_____

_____

_____

_____

_____

_____

_____

_____

_____

_____

_____

Start, Stop, Stick

Throughout your retreat, you may have noticed habits, behaviors, or thought patterns that you want to start, stop, or stick. Review your journal and note them below.

Start: Actions/habits/thought patterns you want to start doing

- _____
- _____
- _____
- _____

Stop: Actions/habits/thought patterns you want to stop doing

- _____
- _____
- _____
- _____

Stick: Actions/habits/thought patterns you want to continue

- _____
- _____
- _____
- _____

What do you think your life will be like once you've shifted your habits and actions based on your Start, Stop, and Stick reflections?

_____
_____
_____

Learned, Loved, Let Go

It's natural to have moments of learning, loving, and letting go throughout a retreat. Review your journal and note your findings below.

Learned: What I learned on my retreat

- _____
- _____
- _____
- _____

Loved: What I loved on my retreat

- _____
- _____
- _____
- _____

Let Go: What I let go of on my retreat

- _____
- _____
- _____
- _____

How have your learned, loved, and let go revelations shifted your inner state?

_____

_____

_____

_____

Unanswered Questions

Take a moment to reflect on any unanswered questions or things you're really not sure about that came up during your retreat. What do you feel is still left to discover or figure out?

_____

_____

_____

_____

_____

_____

_____

_____

_____

_____

_____

_____

_____

_____

_____

_____

_____

_____

_____

_____

_____

_____

Closing Ritual

Take a moment to close your retreat with an activity that connects you one last time to the space, to yourself, and to your personal retreat experience intention. The following are potential ideas, but feel free to choose what feels most aligned and meaningful to you. You can refer back to the "Activity Inspiration" (page 14) and "Opening Ritual" (page 25) for more ideas.

- ☐ Body scan
- ☐ Breathing exercise
- ☐ Centering activity
- ☐ Grounding activity
- ☐ Meditation
- ☐ Walk
- ☐ Yoga
- ☐ Other: _____
- ☐ Other: _____
- ☐ Other: _____
- ☐ Other: _____

Closing Reflections

Spend a moment connecting with your body, mind, and spirit. Notice what thoughts and emotions surface in each area.

Mind: What thoughts are running through your mind right now? Any fears, excitements, or questions to note?

_____

_____

_____

_____

_____

Body: How are you feeling inside? What emotions are just below the surface waiting to come up?

_____

_____

_____

_____

_____

Spirit: What messages does your soul have for you?

_____

_____

_____

_____

Closing Love Letter

Write a love letter to yourself to close out the sacred container of your retreat experience.

Dear _____,

_____

_____

_____

_____

_____

_____

_____

_____

_____

_____

_____

_____

_____

_____

_____

_____

_____

_____

_____

_____

_____

Love, _____

Checkout Checklist

- [ ] Pack

- [ ] Clean

- [ ] If applicable, turn on and reset clocks

- [ ] Return the space to the way it was

- [ ] Take one last moment to breathe in that silence

- [ ] Thank yourself for making the time

- [ ] Pat yourself on the back and give yourself a hug: *I was brave. I did it!*

- [ ] Turn your phone back on (but take some time before checking all your messages!)

- [ ] Get in touch with your trusted friends and loved ones to let them know how you're feeling

One-Word Closer

One word to describe how you are feeling right now:

_____

Trust in Divine Timing

RETREAT
REFLECTIONS
After Your Retreat

Time to Review & Reflect

Timing: A few days after your retreat.

Once you've had time for integration, set aside some time to journal and record your reflections.

This section contains the following suggested prompts for journaling:

- Biggest Insights
- Reoccurring Themes
- Overall Experience
- Actionable Insights
- Accountability & Support
- Celebrate!
- Final Retreat Reflections

Biggest Insights

What were the most profound insights from your retreat experience?

- _____
- _____
- _____
- _____
- _____
- _____
- _____
- _____
- _____
- _____

Take a moment to reflect on your insights. What themes or patterns do you notice?

_____
_____
_____
_____
_____
_____
_____
_____
_____
_____
_____

Reoccurring Themes

What themes came up for you throughout the retreat?

- _____
- _____
- _____
- _____
- _____
- _____
- _____
- _____
- _____
- _____

Why do you feel these themes are so prominent for you?

_____
_____
_____
_____
_____
_____
_____
_____
_____
_____
_____

Overall Experience

How would you describe your retreat experience overall?

_____

_____

_____

_____

_____

_____

_____

How would you recount your retreat experience to people you love and trust?

_____

_____

_____

_____

_____

_____

_____

_____

_____

_____

_____

Actionable Insights

Actionable insights are the clear next steps you'll take away from your retreat experience. List what you'll do next or change moving forward based on the insights you had during your retreat.

- _____
- _____
- _____
- _____

How do your actionable insights make you feel? Which insights feel easy to act upon? Which insights do you need support to follow up on?

_____
_____
_____
_____
_____
_____
_____
_____
_____
_____
_____
_____
_____
_____
_____

Accountability & Support

It is important to take the insights gathered during your retreat and put them into motion. Revisit your actionable insights again in the future to keep them top of mind.

I'm committing to check in and review my actionable insights on:

Date _____

✧ *Tip: Put this date in your digital calendar or planner.*

I will share my actionable insights with my trusted friend/accountability partner:

Name _____ *Date* _____

Tip: Set yourself a digital reminder or alarm for this.

Celebrate!

Your commitment to your personal retreat journey is a huge accomplishment. Take a moment now to soak in the celebration and describe below what you will do later to honour this very big deal!

_____

_____

_____

_____

_____

_____

Final Retreat Reflections

What did this retreat mean to you?

_____

_____

_____

_____

_____

_____

What do you feel will be the most lasting changes that result from this retreat?

_____

_____

_____

_____

_____

_____

_____

My next retreat is planned for:

_____

_____

_____

When you pause and
reflect inward, may
you experience
the magnificence of
your heart's wisdom.

Tonya & Jill

About the Authors

Tonya Darlington

Tonya is the creator of My Retreat Journey (myretreatjourney.ca), where she shares resources to support living a life of abundance in peace, pleasure, and play. Tonya can be found in Dartmouth, Nova Scotia, where she loves to cycle and kayak with her son. She is passionate about supporting women on their healing journey and is a student at the Institute for the Study of Somatic Sex Education.

Jill Pyle

Jill is co-founder of Goddess Provisions (goddessprovisions.com), a community that provides resources and tools for people looking to connect with their divine feminine nature, deepen their spiritual practice, and journey within. Through cosmic downloads, she is guided to create offerings that help raise the vibration of the planet and push the consciousness evolution movement forward. With one foot in the business world and one in the spirit realm, she has a knack for making ancient wisdom and esoteric practices accessible and fit for the modern goddess. Jill is the author of *The Sacred Self-Care Oracle* and co-author of *The Sacred Cycles Oracle* and *The Sacred Cycles Journal*. Find Jill's latest offerings at jillpyle.com.

Oracles to Guide You

THE SACRED CYCLES ORACLE and THE SACRED CYCLES JOURNAL

Deepen your relationship with the Moon cycle, your body, and the rhythms of Earth's Sacred Cycles.

THE SACRED SELF-CARE ORACLE

Find inspiration for creating self-care rituals that will nourish your mind, body, and spirit.

Find these and many other oracle decks and books in the Goddess Provisions Boutique at:

boutique.goddessprovisions.com

Hay House Titles of Related Interest

YOU CAN HEAL YOUR LIFE, the movie,
starring Louise Hay & Friends
(available as an online streaming video)
www.hayhouse.com/louise-movie

THE SHIFT, the movie,
starring Dr. Wayne W. Dyer
(available as an online streaming video)
www.hayhouse.com/the-shift-movie

✳   ✳   ✳

The Sacred Cycles Journal
by Jill Pyle, Em Dewey & Cidney Bachert

3 Minute Positivity Journal
by Kristin Butler

Trust Your Vibes Guided Journal
by Sonia Choquette

Positive Manifestation Journal
by The Hay House Editors

The Gift of Gratitude
by Louise Hay

All of the above are available at your local bookstore,
or may be ordered by contacting Hay House.

✳   ✳   ✳

MEDITATE.
VISUALIZE.
LEARN.

Get the **Empower *You***
Unlimited Audio *Mobile App*

Get unlimited access to the entire Hay House audio library!

You'll get:

- 500+ inspiring and life-changing **audiobooks**

- 200+ ad-free **guided meditations** for sleep, healing, relaxation, spiritual connection, and more

- Hundreds of audios **under 20 minutes** to easily fit into your day

- **Exclusive content** *only* for subscribers

- No credits, **no limits**

New audios added every week!

 ⭐⭐⭐⭐⭐ **I ADORE this app.**
I use it almost every day. Such a blessing. – Aya Lucy Rose

Scan me with your phone camera!

HAY HOUSE

TRY FOR FREE!
Go to: hayhouse.com/listen-free

We hope you enjoyed this Hay House book. If you'd like to receive our online catalog featuring additional information on Hay House books and products, or if you'd like to find out more about the Hay Foundation, please contact:

Hay House, Inc., P.O. Box 5100, Carlsbad, CA 92018-5100
(760) 431-7695 or (800) 654-5126
(760) 431-6948 (fax) or (800) 650-5115 (fax)
www.hayhouse.com® • www.hayfoundation.org

———

Published in Australia by: Hay House Australia Pty. Ltd.,
18/36 Ralph St., Alexandria NSW 2015
Phone: 612-9669-4299 • *Fax:* 612-9669-4144
www.hayhouse.com.au

Published in the United Kingdom by: Hay House UK, Ltd.,
The Sixth Floor, Watson House, 54 Baker Street, London W1U 7BU
Phone: +44 (0)20 3927 7290 • *Fax:* +44 (0)20 3927 7291
www.hayhouse.co.uk

Published in India by: Hay House Publishers India,
Muskaan Complex, Plot No. 3, B-2, Vasant Kunj, New Delhi 110 070
Phone: 91-11-4176-1620 • *Fax:* 91-11-4176-1630
www.hayhouse.co.in

———

Access New Knowledge.
Anytime. Anywhere.

Learn and evolve at your own pace
with the world's leading experts.

www.hayhouseU.com